GRADING AND GROUP WORK

How do I assess individual learning when students work together?

Susan M.
BROOKHART

 Alexandria, VA USA

ASCD
Website: www.ascd.org
E-mail: books@ascd.org

ASCD | arias™
www.ascdarias.org

PAPERBACK ISBN: 978-1-4166-1705-1   ASCD product #SF113073
Also available as an e-book (see Books in Print for the ISBNs).

Library of Congress Cataloging-in-Publication Data
Brookhart, Susan M.
  Grading and group work : how do I assess individual learning when students work together? / Susan M. Brookhart.
      pages cm
  Includes bibliographical references.
  ISBN 978-1-4166-1705-1 (pbk. : alk. paper) 1. Group work in education. 2. Grading and marking (Students) 3. Educational tests and measurements. 4. Educational evaluation. I. Title.
  LB1032.B726 2013
  371.395—dc23
                              2013020741

21 20 19 18 17 16 15 14 13   1 2 3 4 5 6 7 8 9 10

GRADING AND GROUP WORK

How do I assess individual learning when students work together?

Want to earn a free ASCD Arias e-book?
Your opinion counts! Please take 2–3 minutes to give
us your feedback on this publication. All survey
respondents will be entered into a drawing to
win an ASCD Arias e-book.

Click here or type in this web location:
www.ascd.org/ariasfeedback

Thank you!

Does Group *Work* Have to Mean Group *Grades*?

The students in Ms. Smith's 5th grade science class are investigating the effect of watering schedules on the germination and growth of lima bean plants. Working in five groups of four, students develop hypotheses, design and set up experiments, collect data, create tables and graphs depicting their results, and draw conclusions. As a culminating task, each group writes a report and briefly presents its findings to the class. Ms. Smith then leads a class discussion examining the similarities and differences among the groups' work and reviewing what everyone has learned.

Now it's time for grading. But how, exactly, *should* Ms. Smith grade her students on this project? If grades are merely intended to reflect what students *do,* then she can just give higher grades to the more cooperative and industrious groups and lower grades to the less cooperative and industrious groups. But cooperativeness and industriousness are process skills. Granted, we want students to learn those skills, and many report cards provide ways for teachers to appraise them. Nevertheless, subject-matter or standards-based grades are supposed to reflect what students *learn* (Brookhart, 2011; O'Connor, 2009). And what students learn should be based on the learning outcomes reflected in the standards or curriculum goals that form the foundation for both instruction and assessment.

Many teachers struggle with the tension between the need to have students work and learn together and the need to provide grades for individual students. Communication and collaboration have always been important learning skills, and they are especially crucial in the 21st century (Partnership for 21st Century Skills, 2011). Cooperative learning is an effective instructional method for a wide variety of learning goals and is one of the best examples to date of the application of educational psychology to educational practice (Johnson & Johnson, 2009).

Many teachers use group work in a general sense, assigning students to collaborate in groups on projects that result in one undifferentiated product. But true cooperative learning requires individual accountability. No matter what kind of cooperative learning or group work you employ, it is important *not* to give group grades (Brookhart, 2011; Kagan, 1995; O'Connor, 2009; Wormeli, 2006).

What's Wrong with Group Grades?

Group grades are a bad idea because they fail to reflect what a grade is supposed to reflect: an individual student's achievement on a learning standard or curricular outcome. That reason in itself should carry the argument. But there's more: group grades can also have unintended harmful consequences that inhibit student learning.

For example, group grades mean that two students who attained the same knowledge and skills but were in different groups could receive different grades. Given the role that past successes and failures play in students' decisions on how much effort to put forth in a given class or subject, the consequences of such misinformation can be long-standing.

In addition, giving group grades deprives students of individual, actionable feedback on their work or on their understanding of the content. In effect, group grades stop the action in a student's learning trajectory, conveying the message that getting the project done is more important than the learning that results from the project.

Group grades can also mean that some students in a group feel unwarranted pressure to compensate for fellow group members who either won't or can't do good work. These students may find it easier to just do the work for their noncontributing groupmates instead of helping or reasoning with them. Such a situation creates ill will among group members and actually works against the intended purposes of cooperative learning.

Grading Cooperative Learning Versus Group Work

Having established that group grades are a bad idea, the next step is to figure out how to grade students individually for group projects. There are many ways, but each approach falls into one of two general categories of instructional and assessment methods: cooperative learning and group work.

Cooperative Learning

The cooperative learning model builds individual accountability into the requirements for instruction and assessment. Because my focus here is on grading and not on cooperative learning, I won't elaborate on all of the cooperative learning strategies out there. However, I want to emphasize that in true cooperative learning, individuals demonstrate their own learning and receive their own grades. True cooperative learning follows the principles of positive interdependence and individual accountability so that students' learning is affected by both their own and others' work (Johnson & Johnson, 2009). There are many models for cooperative learning, such as the Roundtable cooperative learning structure, in which group members pass around a paper and a pencil and write down their answers in turn. In this way, the learning of all is enhanced by seeing the thinking of each—but the ultimate assessment of what each group member has learned is yet to come (Kagan, 1989).

Cooperative learning strategies can be differentiated to take into account varying student strengths and needs (Schneidewind & Davidson, 2000). For example, teachers can design cooperative learning activities that assign each member of a group distinct learning objectives or criteria for success. The social learning goal may be the same for all group members—say, working productively around a particular topic—but some students may be working on basic concepts while others extend their understanding of more sophisticated concepts. Again, the ultimate assessment of learning is individual.

Group Work

The second method involves building individual assessment opportunities into group work and assessing process skills separately from achievement of learning outcomes. Unlike cooperative learning, which is an instructional strategy, general group work is often intended to serve as both an instructional strategy and an assessment strategy. In the interest of assessing authentic work, teachers often devise a combination of instructional activities and complex performance assessments and then assign them to a group under the umbrella term *group project*. This is where group grades become tempting. Don't give in to that temptation! You don't have to give up your group projects; you just need to figure out how to ascertain what individual group members have *learned* from doing the projects. You can start by following these steps:

1. Ask yourself what it is you want students to learn by engaging in the group project. The answer should relate to one or more state standards or curricular goals.

2. Define precisely the knowledge and skills that students need to be able to complete the group project. The project should tap both learning and process skills and content knowledge and skills. List them separately. If no learning and process skills are required, then the project isn't an effective use of group work. If no content knowledge and skills are required, then the project isn't an effective use of instructional and assessment time.

3. Plan ways to observe and assess (but not grade) the learning and process skills—both individual ("Shawn, make sure to listen as much as you talk in your group") and collective ("I see your group trying hard to make a place for everyone's ideas in your final terrarium plan")—and to give feedback about them.

4. Plan ways to observe and assess individuals' content knowledge and skills. These assessments can be graded.

The key to grading students' work in groups is to separate the development of learning and process skills, which can be assessed both individually and collectively, from the achievement of learning outcomes, which should be assessed and graded individually. It is possible to assess learning along the way while students are still working and learning to do something with support, but the ultimate goal is for students to be able to independently complete tasks that require the knowledge and skills you intended them to learn (Frey, Fisher, & Everlove, 2009).

The following section describes methods for assessing learning and process skills. Remember, these are the skills you assess but do *not* grade. In the section on assessing and grading individual students' achievement (p. 13), I explain how you can plan your assessment of learning and process skills at the same time as you plan your assessment of student learning outcomes.

How Can I Assess Learning and Process Skills?

Some learning and process skills are individual, relating to how a student participates in the group, and some are truly about the dynamics of the group as a whole. Once you have decided on the learning and process skills you want students to develop, select an assessment method that fits. The following sections describe some ways to assess and report these process skills.

Student Reflection on Group Process

At the end of each work session, have students take a minute to reflect on their own contribution to the group's work that day. Use prompts such as "What did your group accomplish today? How did you contribute to the work? What will you need to do to contribute to tomorrow's work?" Students could write their responses on a half-sheet of paper and turn it in to you in the style of an exit ticket, or they could record their comments in a journal.

Rubrics

Using general rubrics for student participation in group work can help define for students what responsible participation looks like. Create rubrics that describe your expectations for group work in the current context, or adapt existing rubrics to your needs. If your district's report card includes scales for learning skills or work habits, then the group participation rubric should align with those. However, do not use group participation rubrics to grade content learning.

Figure 1 shows an example of a simple, general rubric for group participation. It does not fit all contexts—all grade levels, subject areas, and types of group work—but it does illustrate how a rubric can simply and concisely set out for students what their participation should look like and give them a tool for monitoring their own participation. Notice that it is written from a student's point of view.

Give students this rubric before assigning group work, or hand out some sample group participation rubrics they can use to guide them in crafting their own. Consider

FIGURE 1: **Group Participation Rubric**			
Helpful and More	**Helpful**	**Almost Helpful**	**Not Helpful**
• I helped set my group's work goals today and helped keep the group focused and on track.	• I helped set my group's work goals today and stayed focused on them.	• I accepted the work goals that other group members set today.	• I resisted the work goals we set today and got the group off track.
• I contributed something very important to the work we did today.	• I contributed something important to the work we did today.	• I contributed something to the work we did today.	• I didn't contribute anything to the work we did today, or I did contribute but the group had to make me do it
• I listened to other group members today and responded in a helpful way.	• I listened to other group members today.	• I talked too much, or I didn't listen enough to other group members.	• I distracted the group by what I said and did today.

having students role-play what each description looks like in action. I was once assigned to be the "Not Helpful" participant in a role-play. I rummaged through my purse and put on some lipstick as my fellow group members tried to persuade me to pay attention. Students can have fun, but they will also learn how the various roles they play in a group affect the other members of the group.

Once you have introduced group participation rubrics to your class, have students set themselves a personal challenge to be either a "Helpful" or a "Helpful and More" group member each day. At the end of every group work session, have the members of each group take five minutes to reflect together on how they did. Set the expectation that each student will speak for him- or herself ("I was 'Helpful' today because . . ."). Peers can respond—for example, to a group member who thought she was "Not Helpful" ("No, I found it very helpful when you . . .")—but they do not rate or evaluate others. This is a self-reflection and feedback strategy, not a peer evaluation.

Peer Evaluation

When it comes to assessing and discussing group participation, I prefer the self-evaluation and peer feedback method I just described to a more conventional peer evaluation technique. Expecting students to rate one another and discuss differences to consensus without a facilitator or mediator is, at best, ambitious. At worst, it can expose students to uncomfortable situations.

Particularly pernicious—and you will find this sort of thing recommended in books or on the Internet—are anonymous peer evaluations turned in to the teacher, and even worse than *those* are anonymous evaluations that you might use to adjust students' content-area grades. That turns you into the "enforcer," and it encourages students to "rat out" their friends instead of speaking to them directly. What are you supposed to do with an anonymous complaint from one student about another? Whom should you believe?

If you use peer evaluation of group participation, do it with caution, and couple it with your own observations using the same rubric or evaluation form. Peer evaluation of group participation works best with a simple behavioral checklist that students help construct. Figure 2 shows an example of a peer evaluation instrument that a group could use at the end of a work session to discuss its process.

This tool can be used in two different ways. You could hand out copies to all students and ask them to evaluate everyone (including themselves) and then direct the students to discuss their observations in their groups. Alternatively, you could give one copy to each group and ask its members to reach agreement on how they would describe the participation of each group member.

Whichever method you use, communicate clear expectations that students should use the evaluations to decide on their next steps ("I was awesome today; tomorrow I want to do just as well" or "I need to make sure to bring all of my work tomorrow"). Performing an evaluation without using the information it yields is a pointless exercise.

FIGURE 2: **Peer Evaluation of Group Process**			
	Student 1	**Student 2**	**Student 3**
Helped plan the day's goals			
Kept group focused and on track			
Spoke and listened respectfully			
Completed assigned tasks			
[Have students add criteria they think are important.]			

Include directions with this evaluation tool that specify what students should write in the boxes. For example, they could record brief comments, or they could assess one another using

- A checklist (√ or X for *yes,* — or blank for *no*).
- A rating scale (1 through 5).
- A frequency scale (0 = not at all, 1 = sometimes, 2 = frequently).

How Can I Assess and Grade Individual Students' Achievement?

Once you have decided on the learning outcomes you want students to achieve, build in to the group project appropriate individual assessment methods. The following sections describe several effective ways to assess and grade individual achievement of learning outcomes (aligned with curricular or state objectives, goals, or standards) during and after group projects.

Student Reflection on Learning

Asking students to write a reflection on what they learned is not just a good way to assess group process; it can also help you assess and grade individual students' achievement. However, student reflection on learning should differ from student reflection on group process in two ways. First, you should lend more focus to the reflection by providing a clear-cut prompt that cues students to describe specific insights or understandings they gained or particular skills they developed by doing the project. A general answer to the question "What did I learn?" that can be answered many ways (e.g., "I learned that the tides are very important") is not sufficient.

Second, students' responses need to be gradable—on a continuum such as *A* through *F* or Advanced through Below Basic, or on whichever other grading system you use. Like any gradable written project, the student reflection should result in an essay that can be graded with a rubric or other scoring scheme. There will be many ways for students to write a strong answer, but they may also write answers indicating that they did not develop much new knowledge or that they developed misunderstandings.

The key to getting students to demonstrate their understanding of specific content knowledge and skills they learned lies in how you write the reflection prompt. The prompt ought to ask students to make some sort of judgment about the learning—not just rattle off a list of facts.

Here is an example of a project using a reflection prompt.

Sample Project 1: Middle School U.S. History
The Battle of the Little Bighorn

Learning goal: Student understands interaction between Native Americans and white society (e.g., the attitudes and policies of government officials, the U.S. Army, missionaries, and settlers toward Native Americans) (McREL Benchmarks for U.S. History, Standard 19, Level III) (Mid-continent Research for Education and Learning [McREL], 2013a).

Group work: In this project, middle school students conduct research on the Battle of the Little Bighorn, including its causes and effects as well as the details of the event itself. Each group receives a detailed directions sheet that includes research questions. The groups may use one of three formats to report their findings: they may create a "project fair" display on a trifold board (similar to a science fair project); make a series of presentation slides; or produce a written report. In addition to the report, each group is required to summarize its findings for the class in a five-minute oral presentation.

Example of a good reflection prompt: Describe the three most important things you learned about the Battle of the Little Bighorn and the place it holds in the history of the relationship between Native American cultures and the U.S. government. Then share which of those three things surprised you the most, and explain why.

Example of a poor reflection prompt: Summarize what you learned about the Battle of the Little Bighorn.

In this project, many teachers would attempt to assign one grade to the final group report. But no matter which form of presentation the group chose (display, presentation slides, or written report), the content knowledge would have been presented as a product from the group, and it would not be possible to separate the contributions of individual students. Even if that *were* possible, it is not reasonable to conclude that a student who did not personally create a certain portion of the report does not understand that information and its relationship to the other parts of the report. Therefore, a group grade for the final product would not work as an accurate indicator of individual student attainment of the learning goal.

Grading the oral report would give you the opportunity to grade students individually (assuming each group member participates) but only on their oral presentation skills, which are not part of this project's learning goal. A grade for those skills would not provide the right information. And grading the *content* of each individual's part of the oral presentation would run into the same problem that grading each student for the final product would: the oral presentation does not tell you who contributed what information or what additional information any given student learned from doing the project with his or her group.

Thus, the only way to accurately grade individual students' *learning* in this project is to evaluate their responses to the reflection prompt. Let's look at the example of a poor reflection prompt first. This question is ineffective because it taps only recall or, at best, comprehension. It does not require higher-order thinking. In fact, it encourages students to list information point by point and provides no direction on what information to report, how to select it, or how to write about it.

By contrast, a strong reflection question gives students a chance to consolidate their learning and think through its meaning. The example of a good reflection prompt gives students two prioritizing tasks: decide which three things they learned are most important and, of those three, identify which was the most surprising. These tasks require students not only to retain information related to the content standard but also to process it through analysis (breaking the whole of the report into the elements they learned) and evaluation (judging importance and "surprise").

A good reflection prompt functions in the same way as an essay test, with one important difference: whereas a similar question on an essay test would assess students' acquisition of knowledge through their study of assigned materials, the reflection prompt asks students to look at the content through the lens of the group project experience. Students' reflections can still be scored with a rubric, just as they can on essay tests. Here is one example of a rubric you could use.

Scoring Rubric for Reflection Prompt Essays

Advanced: Response shows extended understanding of the interaction between Native Americans and white society, giving an exceptionally detailed explanation of the historical information and its import and an exceptionally clear argument for the choice of information.

Proficient: Response shows understanding of the interaction between Native Americans and white society, giving an accurate explanation of the historical information and its import and a clear argument for the choice of information.

Basic: Response shows limited understanding of the interaction between Native Americans and white society, giving some accurate historical information and some indication of the reason for the choice of information.

Below Basic: Response shows little or no understanding (or a major misunderstanding) of the interaction between

Native Americans and white society, giving inaccurate historical information and no clear reason for the choice of information.

Notice that this rubric is designed for use with a standards-based grading system; similar rubrics could be written for other reporting systems (e.g., for an *A* to *F* continuum). Using this rubric would result in a reportable grade for the student's achievement of the learning goal and provide some general feedback for the student.

Formative assessment opportunities could be built into this project as well, not for grading purposes but to provide additional feedback. Choose a few points during the group-work process where self, peer, or teacher feedback might be valuable. In this project, formative feedback would be helpful when each group settles on a research question, locates sources, produces an outline, or plans its presentation. Students could also use group process self-assessment with a rubric (see Figure 1, p. 9) throughout the project.

Oral Questioning

When you assign groups to share their project results in oral presentations with the class, you can use questioning—both from you and from the rest of the class—to inform your assessment and grading of individual student performance. This method works best when each group's presentation is different. For example, if you tried to question group members during the Little Bighorn oral presentations, all of which covered the same topic, each successive group would have the benefit of hearing the answers given by the previous groups. When groups focus on different topics or aspects of a topic, however, part of their assignment can be to demonstrate their knowledge by responding to questions from you or their classmates.

Here is an example of a project using oral questioning.

Sample Project 2: 6th Grade Science
Simple Machines

Learning goal: Student can explain how the design of simple machines helps reduce the amount of force required to do work and can illustrate ways that simple machines exist in common tools and complex machines (South Carolina Science Academic Standard 6-5, Indicators 6-5.7 and 6-5.8) (South Carolina Department of Education, 2005).

Group work: In this project, students are divided into six groups, each of which must choose a different simple machine to research. An assignment sheet directs students to find at least five examples of the simple machine in use in real life (e.g., in their homes, school, or community). Each group must prepare a class presentation in which it defines its simple machine and presents each real-life example in turn, explaining what work the machine does and how its use reduces the amount of force that the user of the machine needs to exert. For example, a group that has selected the inclined plane as its simple machine may describe and explain the function of wheelchair ramps, playground slides, truck loading ramps, aircraft evacuation slides, and switch-back road construction.

Examples of effective oral questions: What problem can movers solve by using a truck's loading ramp? Why is using the ramp easier for them than lifting a sofa straight up into the truck? Since the sofa weighs the same whether the movers use a ramp or not, how does the ramp make the task easier? [*Questions would be different for each group.*]

Example of ineffective oral question: Tell me about the ramp.

As with the Little Bighorn project, teachers may be tempted to evaluate students individually according to their groups' oral presentations—but as with that project, it would not be easy to tell which student contributed what information, and it would be impossible to define what each student actually learned. Most students likely absorbed content knowledge through the project's process that they did not necessarily contribute to the final group product.

This is where oral questioning comes in. Because each group would be presenting information about a different simple machine, you can use questions to discern individual students' levels of understanding. At the beginning of the project, you should make it clear that you and the rest of the class will be asking questions during each group's presentation and that each student's grade for the presentation will be based on how well he or she answers those questions. Ask questions that require students to think about or explain their reasoning, as the examples of effective questions on page 20 do. Address each question to the student who is speaking at the time, and make sure to ask different questions of different presenters. Evaluate the overall quality of the answers as indicators of understanding—that is, evaluate students' thinking, not their ability to parrot definitions and facts on their feet.

Finally, unless the presentation is especially detailed and long enough to ask numerous questions of each student, I recommend following up the presentations and questioning with a brief student reflection on learning (see preceding section). In order to make a reliable judgment about a student's level of understanding, you need a reasonable amount of information, and a few questions might not be enough for you to confidently evaluate a student's achievement of a learning goal. A written response to a follow-up question (e.g., "Pick one of the examples of inclined planes your group discussed, and explain why you thought it would be a good example to include in the presentation") will give you more information about the student's understanding. You can base your grade for the project on a combination of students' oral and written responses, using a rubric similar to the one shown on pages 17–18.

As with all the projects discussed here, be sure to include formative assessment opportunities for students to get self, peer, or teacher feedback during the course of their learning. Give students time to reflect on their group process, as well, using the rubric in Figure 1 (p. 9).

Multistep Design

For complex group projects, consider using a multistep design that incorporates multiple assessment opportunities, both formative (conducted during earlier phases of the project for the purpose of giving feedback) and summative (conducted during later phases of the project for the purpose of grading). Use this approach for group projects whenever you can. Building in formative assessment opportunities during the course of a project will help students learn more from the process, and feedback can prevent group members from going down an unproductive road and finding out too late that they need to go back and redo a part of their work.

Here is an example of a project employing a multistep design.

Sample Project 3: 8th Grade English
Film Adaptation of Literature

Learning goal: Student can analyze the extent to which a filmed or live production of a story or drama stays faithful to or departs from the text or script, evaluating the choices made by the director or actors (Common Core State Standards for English Language Arts & Literacy, Reading: Literature Standard RL 8.7) (National Governors Association Center for Best Practices [NGA Center] & Council of Chief State School Officers [CCSSO], 2010a).

Group work: After reading the book *Where the Red Fern Grows* by Wilson Rawls, students are asked to analyze the effects on the reader and the viewer, respectively, of choices made by the author of the book and by the director or actors in the movie. In groups of four, they

1. Select and watch a movie adaptation of the book (the 1974 or 2003 version).

2. Choose a character or plot element to focus on, and compare and contrast its presentation in the book with its presentation in the movie.

3. Explain how the differences they have noted may affect the reader/viewer, and what the similarities they have noted (i.e., where the movie stayed true to the book) may say about the effects on the reader/viewer that the filmmakers wanted to retain from the book, and why.

4. Prepare a summary of their findings to present to the class, to be accompanied by clips from the movie.

Examples of assessments to include at different steps in the project:

- At the end of step 1, ask each group to write a one-paragraph statement giving its reasons for choosing the 1974 or 2003 version of the movie. [*formative assessment, completed as a group to gain group feedback from the teacher*]

- At the end of step 2, ask each student to choose one character or plot element, describe its presentation and function in the book and the movie, compare the two presentations, and write a brief "reader response" about his or her own reaction to the book versus the movie. [*formative assessment, completed individually to gain individual feedback from the teacher that might affect group discussion*] [Note: this is a bite-size version of the task the group is undertaking. Getting feedback about their own understanding of this kind of analysis should help students be more productive group members and help you see how student learning is being formed.]

- At the end of step 3 or during step 4, when groups are preparing their presentations, have them turn in an outline that includes the points they want to make and the clips they intend to show in their presentations. [*formative assessment, completed as a group to gain group feedback from the teacher*]
- After groups' presentations are over, have students repeat the individual exercise they did before, choosing one character or plot element (different from the one they wrote about before but included in their group's presentation), describing its presentation and function in the book and the movie, comparing the two presentations, and writing a brief "reader response" about their own reaction to the book versus the movie. [*summative assessment, completed individually for a grade*]

This project will take the groups a while to accomplish. Rather than just cutting students loose and only observing group process for the duration of the project, you can use these various assessment opportunities to keep students on track, provide feedback while students work, and help ensure that the learning outcomes end up being worth the time and effort invested.

These assessments can also inform the final grade. Although you would use the summative task to actually determine students' grades, you can use the results of the assessments you conducted throughout the project to support your decisions; these results provide additional evidence demonstrating that students' work on the summative assessment is not a fluke but a reliable indicator of their achievement. Taken together, the various assessments provide you with an accurate picture of what students know and can do.

Note that during the entire course of this multistep project, you should also be assessing—and having students assess—the group process. For example, students could end every work session by conducting a brief self- or peer reflection on the process, using rubrics, as described in the preceding section on assessing learning and process skills. As you observe students working, you can provide ongoing feedback on the group process. This feedback should help improve both the process and the work that results from it. Just remember that the final grade needs to be based on a task that is aligned with the learning goal—in this case, a Common Core Reading standard.

"Write Your Own Question"

Having students write their own questions can be a highly effective strategy to use both for formative assessment purposes and for grading. Of course, the quality of the questions matters. Students need to be taught how to write "thinking" questions as opposed to just questions of fact. Give students examples of questions that require real thought rather than simple recall, and have them practice writing their own questions until they can create "thinking" questions themselves.

You can easily incorporate this strategy into a multistep group project. Toward the end of the project, as students are putting final touches on their reports or other products, include a step that asks students to think individually about what they are learning from the project and to write down a question that the project has raised for them, helped them answer, or made them curious about. This step should prompt students to explain what led them to ask this question and then to answer their own question by drawing on concepts they learned during the group project. Have students turn in this short paper when their groups turn in their products, or shortly thereafter.

Here is an example of a multistep project that incorporates a "write your own question" step.

Sample Project 4: 4th Grade Math
Model Construction

Learning goal: Student can apply the area and perimeter formulas for rectangles in real-world and mathematical problems (Common Core State Standards for Mathematics Content Standard 4.MD.A.3) and can model with mathematics

(Common Core State Standards for Mathematics Practice MP4) (NGA Center & CCSSO, 2010b).

Group work: In this project, students work in groups to plan and construct a small apartment. The apartment must include a living area, a kitchen/dining area, one bedroom, and a bathroom. Assignment directions specify the steps students should take:

1. Draft a blueprint of the floor plan on paper, labeling the dimensions of each room (realistic dimensions are not necessary; for example, a "room" can measure 6 inches by 8 inches) and making the rooms fit together as a living space. Calculate the perimeter and area of each room.

2. After teacher feedback, revise the blueprint as necessary and transfer it (or glue or tape it) onto cardboard.

3. Measure, cut, and erect "walls" for each of the rooms, again labeling the dimensions and calculating the area and perimeter of each wall. Leave the model open-topped so viewers can see into the rooms. (For students at the basic level, the project might require only that they construct solid walls; more advanced students could be challenged to include windows and doors in their models, calculate their area and perimeter, and subtract their area from the total wall area.)

4. Present the final model, which should include, affixed in each room, the area of the floor to specify the amount of carpet or flooring needed and the area of the walls to specify the amount of wallpaper or other wall covering needed.

5. Decorate the rooms as desired. (The project quality will be assessed according to demonstration of mathematical knowledge and problem-solving and communication skills, not decoration.)

Examples of assessments to include at different steps in the project:

- At the end of step 1, ask each group to assess the mathematical accuracy of its draft blueprint's dimensions and calculations. *[formative assessment, completed as a group to gain group feedback from the teacher]*

- At the end of step 2, ask each student to choose one of the math problems that his or her group completed (e.g., calculation of the perimeter or area of one room) and present it on paper, showing and explaining his or her work. *[formative assessment, completed individually to gain individual feedback from the teacher]*

- After the project is completed, administer a quiz on perimeter and area that includes problems using real-world applications but not those used in the project (e.g., the quiz could ask the student to calculate the area of his or her desktop). *[summative assessment, completed individually for a grade]*

Example of a "write your own question" assessment: In addition to or instead of the final quiz, have students pause when their groups have mostly completed the mathematical part of the project but not yet finished the decorating (between steps 4 and 5). Ask students individually to do one of the following:

- Write down a question that occurred to them during the group work that they needed math to solve (e.g., "How do I find the area of a wall if there's a window in it?" or "How do I find the area of carpet needed to go down a step?") and explain how they solved it.
- Write down a question that occurred to them during the group work that made them think about mathematical ideas (e.g., "How is area related to perimeter?" or "How does the accuracy of my measurements affect my results?") and explain the thinking and reasoning behind asking the question.

Note: students should not be permitted to use the questions that you provide as examples because that would not represent higher-order thinking on their part. Take care not to use up all the "good questions" in your assignment directions.

Notice that this multistep project, like Sample Project 3, includes opportunities for assessment of group process and formative assessment of students' progress toward learning goals in addition to the summative assessment.

It is important to note that because the learning goals of the best multistep group projects involve analysis, evaluation, or creation, the individual graded assessments for these projects should also ask students to demonstrate those skills. Summative assessments don't change the nature of the group work or the learning that was meant to result from it; they simply enable you to evaluate and grade the achievement of individuals rather than a group.

Post-Project Test

Group projects whose principal aim is to teach students facts and concepts are really learning activities—not performance assessments. The best of these kinds of projects harness the power of the group and teach concepts in a dynamic way—for example, by having students role-play a model legislature or portray a live model of an atom by acting out the parts of protons, neutrons, and electrons. But the actual learning goals of these projects aren't for Bianca to act like a great legislator or for Jayden to walk the electron orbit; the goals are for students to grasp the legislative process and to understand atomic structure. Thus, you can't formulate accurate grades by assessing students' participation in these activities; the grading must come after the project, when you assess what students have learned from the activities.

Here is an example of this kind of "learning activity" group project.

Sample Project 5: Middle School World History
New Technology in the Industrial Revolution

Learning goal: Student knows the roles of interchangeable parts and mass production in the Industrial Revolution (McREL Benchmarks for World History, Standard 33, Level III, Benchmark 5, Knowledge/skill statement 2) (McREL, 2013b).

Group work: In this project, students work in groups of five to assemble paper models of hot-air balloons. Every group except one uses the division-of-labor method, in which student 1 cuts balloon bags from construction paper; student 2 cuts baskets from construction paper; student 3 decorates the balloon bags; student 4 measures and cuts strings; and student 5 assembles the whole balloon, connecting the bag to the basket with the strings. The remaining group uses the cottage-industry method, in which each student assembles his or her own balloon in its entirety. After 15 minutes, each group computes how many balloons per worker were assembled using its method. The group work is followed by a class discussion in which students compare and contrast the two production methods (Miller, n.d.).

Gradable measure of students' achievement: Give a test asking questions that align with the project's learning goal. This may be part of a larger unit test that includes other learning goals.

This is an example of a project that makes good use of group time. Working alone, students wouldn't be able to experience firsthand some of the developments of the Industrial Revolution, which is part of the point of the exercise. However, you wouldn't want to grade each student's work in the group as if it were a learning outcome in itself. The learning goal, which is what the grade should reflect, is for students to know about interchangeable parts and mass production. What students did in their groups was experience and demonstrate some of the factors involved in mass production and the use of interchangeable parts, and their grades should reflect what they learned from that experience.

The best way to assess what students learned from these kinds of group learning activities is to administer a test after the project has been completed. The test can include conventional selected-response (multiple-choice) questions, essay questions, problems to solve, or a combination of different types of questions. Plan your test by referring to the learning goal. What kind of test would best indicate student achievement of that goal? Construct the test accordingly, and use it to arrive at each student's grade on the particular learning goals. Of course, a test only measures student achievement as you intend if you plan it properly and write items that truly assess what you have in mind. A complete presentation of test construction is beyond the scope of this writing, but interested readers should consult *Assessment and Grading in Classrooms* (Brookhart & Nitko, 2008).

I have seen a wide variety of "group projects" that basically amount to students gathering facts and then presenting them in some "creative" way—on a poster, in a brochure, through a quiz game . . . you name it. I want to caution you that the kind of activity that has students create posters about the U.S. states or brochures that describe different animals is usually not the best use of group time. All of these *look* like projects but are actually fact-finding assignments— and sometimes classroom decoration assignments. It is something of a waste of students' brainpower to have them work together toward such an educationally thin outcome. A further drawback is that despite many teachers' assumption that students "learn" the facts they report in their presentations and *Jeopardy!* games, these types of projects are more about accurate copying of facts than about committing content to memory. Students don't necessarily retain learning from these assignments.

That said, these projects can have their place. Learning together is valuable, and producing visual reminders of learning can help create the classroom atmosphere you want for a given unit of study. And, as with the other projects discussed here, you can easily assess group process during the course of such a project. Keep in mind, though, that a test administered after the project is completed is the only way to accurately ascertain individual students' attainment of the learning goal.

Here is an example of this kind of project.

Sample Project 6: Elementary School Health
How to Stay Healthy

Learning goal: Student knows how to maintain and promote personal health (McREL Benchmarks for Health, Standard 7, Level II) (McREL, 2013c).

Group work: In this project, students work in groups to create brochures to put in a doctor's office that describe a common disease or health problem affecting children and include three things that can be done to prevent it. For example, a brochure on the common cold could include the preventive actions of washing hands, covering sneezes, and getting plenty of sleep.

Gradable measure of students' achievement: Give a test asking questions that align with the project's learning goal. This may be part of a larger unit test that includes other learning goals.

Although this project merely requires looking up some facts and organizing them into a brochure, it serves as an enjoyable way for younger students to learn some of the information involved in the learning goal. The learning goal is broader than the project's products—essentially, lists of disease-prevention strategies—but talking together about the importance of maintaining personal hygiene and health will help develop students' disposition to do so. A post-project test would tap this broader outcome, whereas grading the brochures would just indicate whether students were able to look up and transcribe three facts related to one disease.

How Can I Adapt Group Projects to Enable Individual Grading?

I hope that you find the suggestions I offer here helpful. Most teachers I know who give group grades have a nagging feeling about it; they don't really want to do it, but they aren't sure how else to come up with a grade while staying true to the learning intentions for the group work.

If this is true for you, another issue may arise. You may have some group projects in your teaching repertoire that you and your students enjoy. If they are good group projects, you shouldn't have to give them up. You should, however, adapt them to enable individual rather than group grading.

I recommend that you proceed in two steps. First, evaluate the project and make sure it takes advantage of the power of group learning and involves higher-order thinking and interactive discussion—and isn't just an exercise in copying facts or decorating the room. If your project is a thin one, you can either discard or revise it. Often, it is possible to add a higher-order thinking or group discussion–worthy dimension to a surface-level project. For example, instead of having students make posters displaying facts about a given U.S. state, ask them to look up relevant facts—population, governance, education, weather, geography, natural resources, products and services, and so on—and then envision what it might be like to live in that state. Students could create both a poster and a TV or radio spot enticing people or businesses to move to that state.

Once you are sure that your group project is worthy of the time and energy it will take, follow these steps:

1. Ask yourself what it is you want students to learn by engaging in the group project. The project should be clearly aligned with one or more state standards or curricular goals.

2. Define precisely the knowledge and skills that students need to be able to complete the group project. The project should tap both learning and process skills (which should be assessed to provide feedback) and content knowledge and skills (which should be assessed and graded for individual students). List them separately.

3. Plan ways to observe, assess, and provide feedback on (but not grade) the learning and process skills, using the suggestions offered here to guide you.

4. Plan ways to observe, assess, and provide feedback on the content knowledge and skills described in the learning goals. Then plan ways to observe, assess, and grade individuals' final achievement of those learning goals.

The decisions you make as you plan assessments for your group project will depend on what sort of project you have. Is it a short project, amenable to grading a student reflection, oral questions, or a brief post-project test or quiz? Or is it a longer, multistep project that needs several assessment opportunities built in along the way? Revise your project accordingly.

ENCORE

GRADING AND GROUP WORK

Whichever kinds of group projects you use in your classroom, it is important to resist giving group grades. Use the ideas and strategies offered in the following questions, tips, and resources to help you find effective ways to grade the learning of individual students.

REFLECTION QUESTIONS

◯ What group projects do I currently use? How do I grade the student learning that results from these projects?

◯ If I currently give group grades for any of my projects, how can I best revise the project and its assessment plan to result in individual grades? How can I identify criteria for student learning that align with the standard(s) or curricular objective(s) that this project is meant to assess?

◯ Does my district's report card include scales for learning skills, work habits, or citizenship? If not, which learning and process skills in this project are most important to observe and provide feedback on?

QUICK WINS

If your students are used to getting group grades, start small. The following steps will help you get started.

◯ 1. Select one project that is not very complex, and follow one of the assessment strategies described on pages 13–34, or consult the section titled "How Can I Adapt Group Projects to Enable Individual Grading?" (pp. 34–36). Tell students at the outset that you will assess both their learning and process skills and what they learn from doing the project.

◯ 2. After both the project (including formative feedback on learning and process skills) and the graded assessment of learning are completed, engage students in either a journal-write or a brief class discussion to reflect on their experience getting individual grades for learning accomplished through group work. Be careful not to phrase your question or prompt in a way that leads students to believe they will be "voting" on how they should be graded. You are interested in students' perceptions of what their grades mean and how accurate and fair they are.

◯ 3. Use the feedback you receive as you plan future individual assessments of group work. Research suggests that students do not perceive group grades as fair, so most students will likely welcome individual grades (Conway,

Kember, Sivan, & Wu, 1993). If some of your students *do* express a preference for group grades, do not let that tempt you to use them again. Rather, look for the reasons behind students' complaints. Most commonly, these will include a mismatch between what students learned during the group work and what you tested them on or a misunderstanding at the outset that students would be assessed individually on their learning.

If you use a complex culminating group project for a semester or course, you may already have built in some individual grading to the project. If there is one final "big kahuna" grade for the entire project, though, try incorporating additional assessment opportunities into the multistep project (see also the section titled "Multistep Design," p. 22):

◯ 1. Identify natural places throughout the course of the project where you could include opportunities for formative feedback on learning to both individuals and groups. If these assessment opportunities are not fairly frequent, tweak the assignment directions to build them in.

◯ 2. Identify natural places throughout the course of the project work where you could include opportunities for feedback on learning and process skills.

◯ 3. Consider augmenting the big final grade, which assesses the entire body of knowledge and skills covered by the project, with one or more grades that evaluate smaller chunks of content knowledge or skills. Build in opportunities for these small summative assessments of content close to the time when students are actually learning that content.

RESOURCES FOR GROUP PROJECTS

There are numerous online resources to help you design robust group projects and accompanying assessments. I want to offer a caveat up front, though: no matter how reputable a website or resource is or how great its ideas, you still need to cast a critical eye on its suggested projects and assessment plans to make sure they suit your purposes, align with your standard or curricular objective, and follow the rules for good assessment design. That said, the following resources should help you conceive and design worthwhile group projects.

○ For general projects: Buck Institute for Education, Project-Based Learning (www.bie.org) and Edutopia (www.edutopia.org/project-based-learning)

○ For science projects: National Aeronautics and Space Administration (http://spaceplace.nasa.gov)

○ For social studies projects: Smithsonian Source: Resources for Teaching American History (www. smithsoniansource.org)

References

Brookhart, S. M. (2011). *Grading and learning: Practices that support student achievement.* Bloomington, IN: Solution Tree.

Brookhart, S. M., & Nitko, A. J. (2008). *Assessment and grading in classrooms.* Upper Saddle River, NJ: Pearson.

Conway, R., Kember, D., Sivan, A., & Wu, M. (1993). Peer assessment of an individual's contribution to a group project. *Assessment & Evaluation in Higher Education, 18,* 45–56.

Frey, N., Fisher, D., & Everlove, S. (2009). *Productive group work.* Alexandria, VA: ASCD.

Johnson, D. W., & Johnson, R. T. (2009). An educational psychology success story: Social interdependence theory and cooperative learning. *Educational Researcher, 38,* 365–379.

Kagan, S. (1989). The structural approach to cooperative learning. *Educational Leadership, 47*(4), 12–15.

Kagan, S. (1995). Group grades miss the mark. *Educational Leadership, 52*(8), 68–71.

Mid-continent Research for Education and Learning (McREL). (2013a). *McREL Compendium of Content Standards and Benchmarks for K–12 Education, Benchmarks for U.S. History, Standard 19, Level III (grades 7–8).* Retrieved from www2.mcrel.org/compendium

McREL. (2013b). *McREL Compendium of Content Standards and Benchmarks for K–12 Education, Benchmarks for World History, Standard 33, Level III (grades 7–8), Benchmark 5, Knowledge and Skill Statement 2.* Retrieved from www2.mcrel.org/compendium

McREL. (2013c). *McREL Compendium of Content Standards and Benchmarks for K–12 Education, Benchmarks for Health, Standard 7, Level II (grades 3–5).* Retrieved from www2.mcrel.org/compendium

Miller, R. (n.d.). *Social studies group projects: Economics.* Retrieved from www.ehow.com/info_7976396_social-studies-group-projects.html

National Governors Association Center for Best Practices (NGA Center) & Council of Chief State School Officers (CCSSO). (2010a). *Common Core State Standards for English Language Arts & Literacy in History/Social Studies, Science, and Technical Subjects.* Washington, DC: Author. Retrieved from www.corestandards.org/ELA-Literacy

NGA Center & CCSSO. (2010b). *Common Core State Standards for Mathematics.* Washington, DC: Author. Retrieved from www.corestandards.org/Math

O'Connor, K. (2009). *How to grade for learning K–12* (3rd ed.). Thousand Oaks, CA: Corwin.

Partnership for 21st Century Skills. (2011). *Framework for 21st century learning.* Washington, DC: Author.

Schneidewind, N., & Davidson, E. (2000). Differentiating cooperative learning. *Educational Leadership, 58*(1), 24–27.

South Carolina Department of Education. (2005). *South Carolina Science Academic Standards, grade 6: Conservation of energy.* Columbia, SC: Author. Retrieved from http://ed.sc.gov/agency/se/Teacher-Effectiveness/Standards-and-Curriculum/documents/sciencestandards-nov182005_001.pdf

Wormeli, R. (2006). *Fair isn't always equal: Assessing and grading in the differentiated classroom.* Portland, ME: Stenhouse.

Related Resources

At the time of publication, the following ASCD resources were available (ASCD stock numbers appear in parentheses). For up-to-date information about ASCD resources, go to www.ascd.org. You can search the complete archives of Educational Leadership at http://www.ascd.org/el.

ASCD EDge®

Exchange ideas and connect with other educators interested in various topics, including Assessment and Grading, Effective Feedback, and Formative Assessment on the social networking site ASCD EDge at http://ascdedge.ascd.org.

Print Products

Advancing Formative Assessment in Every Classroom: A Guide for Instructional Leaders by Susan M. Brookhart and Connie M. Moss (#109031)

Checking for Understanding: Formative Assessment Techniques for Your Classroom by Nancy E. Frey and Douglas B. Fisher (#107023)

Classroom Assessment and Grading That Work by Robert J. Marzano (#106006)

Formative Assessment Strategies for Every Classroom: An ASCD Action Tool by Susan M. Brookhart (#111005)

How to Create and Use Rubrics for Formative Assessment and Grading by Susan M. Brookhart (#112001)

How to Give Effective Feedback to Your Students by Susan M. Brookhart (#108019)

What Teachers Really Need to Know About Formative Assessment by Laura Greenstein (#110017)

ASCD PD Online® Courses

Assessment: Designing Performance Assessments, 2nd Ed. (#PD11OC108)

Formative Assessment: Deepening Understanding (#PD11OC101)

Formative Assessment: The Basics (#PD09OC69)

For more information: send e-mail to member@ascd.org; call 1-800-933-2723 or 703-578-9600, press 2; send a fax to 703-575-5400; or write to Information Services, ASCD, 1703 N. Beauregard St., Alexandria, VA 22311-1714 USA.

About the Author

Susan M. Brookhart, PhD, is an independent educational consultant based in Helena, Montana, and is Coordinator of Assessment and Evaluation for the School of Education at Duquesne University. She is the author or coauthor of several books, including ASCD's *How to Give Effective Feedback to Your Students, How to Assess Higher-Order Thinking Skills in Your Classroom, Advancing Formative Assessment in Every Classroom,* and *Learning Targets: Helping Students Aim for Understanding in Today's Lesson.* She may be reached at susanbrookhart@bresnan.net.